AUSTRALIA'S
WILDFLOWERS

Photography by Ken Stepnell

Text by Dalys Newman

WOOLLAHRA

PREVIOUS PAGE: Flame heath *(Styphelia behrii)* is one of 15 attractive species found in areas of Victoria, South Australia and New South Wales. Tubular flowers of pink, red, yellow, cream or green grow from the base of the leaves.

ABOVE: Native to Western Australia, the beautiful rose of the west *(Eucalyptus macrocarpa)* is a straggly shrub growing to over 3 metres. The spectacular red flowers are up to 1 centimetre in diameter and contrast strikingly with the silvery grey leaves.

BELOW LEFT: The scarlet flowering gum *(Eucalyptus ficifolia)* bears large clusters of scarlet or orange flowers in summer and autumn, followed by enormous urn-shaped seed capsules.

BELOW RIGHT: White-flowering grey mallee *(Eucalyptus socialis)* is native to areas of inland Australia.

OPPOSITE: New South Wales floral emblem, the waratah *(Telopea speciosissima)*, is found mainly on the coastal plains and tablelands of this state. Its botanical name means 'beautiful plant seen from afar', and its striking flowerheads can easily be spotted from a distance in the Australian bush.

OPPOSITE: The intense royal blue flowers of common dampiera *(Dampiera linearis)* are said to resemble a hand. Native to Western Australia, this plant is often seen massed along roadsides in country areas.

ABOVE: Catspaw *(Anigozanthos humilis)*, the most common of the kangaroo paws, is found in open forests throughout most of Western Australia. It is particularly evident after bushfires.

CENTRE: Spring-flowering, the black kangaroo paw *(Macropidia fuliginosa)* is found in heath and mallee communities in eastern Western Australia. It has 50 centimetre long, blue-green, strap-like leaves and greenish-yellow flowers with black sooty hairs.

RIGHT: One of Australia s best known wildflowers, the red and green kangaroo paw *(Anigozanthos manglesii)* is the floral emblem of Western Australia. The exotic, bird-attracting *Anigozanthos* species are characteristic of the many unusual plants of the Australian continent, which has been so long separated from other land masses.

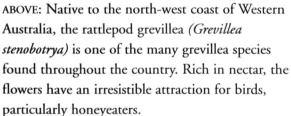

ABOVE: Native to the north-west coast of Western Australia, the rattlepod grevillea *(Grevillea stenobotrya)* is one of the many grevillea species found throughout the country. Rich in nectar, the flowers have an irresistible attraction for birds, particularly honeyeaters.

ABOVE RIGHT: Fuchsia mallee *(Eucalyptus forrestiana)* grows to about six metres. This gum species has very distinctive 'pendulous' red bell-like flowers that appear during spring and summer.

RIGHT: One of over a hundred species of daviesia, commonly known as bitter peas, that occur through-out the country, *Daviesia inflata* is found in Western Australia.

OPPOSITE: White-flowered rhodanthe, yellow angianthus and pink mulla mullas make a delightful spring display in the goldfields of Western Australia. After rains, dry inland areas of Australia become alive with a colourful kaleidoscope of wildflowers.

OVERLEAF: A typical scene of wildflowers in Western Australia during the spring season.

ABOVE: Heath-leaf banksia *(Banksia ericifolia)* is one of the most attractive of all banksias. Named after botanist Sir Joseph Banks, there are about 70 species of banksia, found in most environments including the tropics, sub-alpine, coast and desert areas.

ABOVE RIGHT: Growing to 3 metres in height, hooker's banksia *(Banksia hookeriana)* flowers from April to October. Banksias vary in size from prostrate shrubs, in which the flower spike arises from the ground, to large trees.

CENTRE RIGHT: Named after Queen Victoria, the woolly orange banksia *(Banksia victoriae)* is summer flowering and native to Western Australia. Banksias are thought to have existed for over 40 million years. The Australian Aborigines used the nectar from the flowers as part of their diet.

RIGHT: The striking cut-leaf banksia *(Banksia praemorsa)* is also a Western Australian native. Over 80 per cent of the banksia genus occurs in the southern areas of this state.

LEFT: Known as pineapple bush or drumsticks *(Dasypogon bromeliifolius)*, this plant is found only in Western Australia. Belonging to the grass tree family, these unusual natives have stiff, grass-like leaves and small creamy white flowers that grow in dense globular heads on top of long flower stems. They flower during spring and summer and are a popular florists' flower because of their striking appearance.

BELOW: Native to South Australia and Victoria, *Ixodia achilleoides* is a member of the daisy family, commonly occurring after bush fires in high rainfall areas. Its sprays of white, papery flowers, appearing in summer, are also popular with florists, often being used in dried flower arrangements. The flowers, growing in terminal clusters on 50 centimetre stems, can be easily dyed and are durable and long-lasting.

OPPOSITE: Common heath *(Epacris impressa)* is native to areas of Victoria, New South Wales, Tasmania and South Australia. The flowers, which can be pink, red or white, appear from autumn through to spring.

BELOW: Native to Western Australia, cowslip orchids *(Caladenia flava)* have broad, hairy leaves and yellow flowers with red on the stems. These ground orchids flower mainly in spring.

RIGHT: An epiphytic orchid, the spider orchid *(Dendrobium tetragonum)* is native to areas of New South Wales and Queensland. There are over 50 species of epiphytic orchids in Australia, growing on both trees and rocks and favouring rainforest conditions.

CENTRE RIGHT: The spring-flowering native orchid *Dendrobium gracillimum* is found in rainforests, sclerophyll forests, stream-side areas, rocky crevices and scree.

BOTTOM RIGHT: Among the most beautiful of Australia's orchids, the salmon sun orchid *(Thelymitra rubra)* takes its name from the fact that it opens and closes with the sun. Spring-flowering, it is native to Victoria, Tasmania, South Australia and New South Wales.

OPPOSITE: The winter-flowering Cooktown orchid *(Dendrobium bigibbum)* is native to northern Queensland and the floral emblem of that state. It grows in stunted coastal scrub, monsoon thickets and open habitats and is threatened in some areas due to extensive harvesting. White, lilac, mauve or magenta flowers, up to 5 centimetres across, are borne on 40 centimetre long racemes.

ABOVE: Alpine groundsel *(Senecio pectinatus)* is a member of the daisy family found in the higher alpine areas of New South Wales, Tasmania and Victoria. Summer-flowering, it is one of 40 native species which are annuals or perennials and range from small herbs to bushy shrubs.

BELOW: Mainly found in Western Australia, woodbridge poison *(Isotoma hypocrateriformis)* is a small herb with delicate mauve or white flowers that appear in spring.

ABOVE: *Pimelea ferruginea* belongs to the same family as the exotic daphne. Found in Western Australia, it is a pink-flowered bushy shrub growing to about 1 metre tall.

CENTRE: Masses of small white to pink flowers almost obscure the leaves of grampians thryptomene *(Thryptomene calycina)* during winter and spring. There are over 40 species of thryptomene, with the greatest number found in Western Australia.

BELOW: Red lechenaultia *(Lechenaultia formosa)* is one of about 20 species of this genus found in Western Australia. Flowering from spring through to autumn, the blooms can be scarlet, orange or red.

OPPOSITE: Native to South Australia and Western Australia, silver goodenia *(Goodenia tripartita)* is a member of an attractive group of plants widely distributed throughout the country. It was previously known as *Goodenia affinis.*

LEFT: The Swan River pea bush *(Brachysema celsianum)*, found in south-western Australia, flowers mainly in spring. A low, scrambling shrub, it has rounded leaves and typical bright red pea flowers with very large wings, about 25 millimetres long. Honey-eating birds are attracted to its nectar. There are 16 species in this genus, all of which are prostrate to medium shrubs and found only in Western Australia.

BELOW: Spring-flowering brush heath *(Brachyloma ericoides)* is found growing in sandy light soils in areas of Victoria, New South Wales and South Australia.

ABOVE: The dark pink flowers of tetratheca *(Tetratheca thymifolia)* appear in abundance during spring. Native to Victoria, New South Wales and Queensland, this plant grows to 1 metre in height.

ABOVE LEFT: Shiny tea-tree *(Leptospermum nitidum)* makes a dramatic addition to bushland in Victoria and Tasmania. There are over 40 species of tea-trees, found in all states of Australia.

CENTRE LEFT: Flowering from late winter to spring, native daphne *(Eriostemon myoporoides)* is found in New South Wales, Victoria and Queensland. Belonging to the waxflower family, these pretty plants with their starry, five-petalled flowers have been longtime garden favourites.

LEFT: The grass-leaved trigger plant *(Stylidium graminifolium)* has a unique mechanism for ensuring fertilisation. When an insect touches the column created by the filaments of the stamens and the pistil, it springs across and secures the insect. In its struggle for freedom the insect removes some of the pollen which it then carries to other flowers.

LEFT: Floral emblem of the Northern Territory, Sturt's desert rose *(Gossypium sturtianum)* is also found in arid regions in South Australia, New South Wales and Queensland. Its delicate hibiscus-like flowers appear in winter and spring and the plants contain a substance which is toxic to non-ruminant animals.

LEFT: Fairy aprons *(Utricularia dichotoma)* are native to New South Wales, Victoria, South Australia, Western Australia and Tasmania. Dainty lilac to purple flowers appear from spring through summer around fresh water swamps, in bog areas and near wet rocks. They often grow beneath the water surface, developing small bladders which trap and digest marine life.

LEFT: Found in the alpine areas of Victoria, Tasmania and New South Wales, snow daisies *(Celmisia longifolia)* are perennial herbs. They carpet alpine slopes in summer with their narrow silvery leaves and large white, yellow-centred flowers.

BOTTOM LEFT: The small fluffy pink flowers of mat mulla mulla *(Ptilotus obovatus)* dramatically contrast with the parched red earth of inland Australia. There are over 100 species of these extremely drought resistant, spring-flowering plants found throughout the mainland.

OPPOSITE: Soft mauve pea *(Gompholobium villosum)* is a spring-flowering plant native to Western Australia. There are about 26 species in this genus and they produce some of the largest of the Australian pea flowers. Flowers come in shades of delicate lemon yellow to red and violet blue.

OPPOSITE: The bright yellow flowers of desert phebalium *(Phebalium glandulosum)* appear in late winter and spring. Native to areas of Queensland, New South Wales, South Australia and Victoria, these plants are members of the boronia family.

RIGHT: The striking blue pea-flowers of thorny hovea *(Hovea acanthoclada)* brighten the winter landscape of Western Australia. The genus was named after Anthony Hove, a Polish collector sent out by Sir Joseph Banks from Kew Gardens in England in the 1780s.

RIGHT: Cascade everlastings *(Helichrysum secundiflorum)* make a frothy statement in the alpine areas of Victoria, Tasmania and New South Wales. These summer-flowering paper daisies have always been popular for dried flower arrangements. There are over 100 species in this genus, some of which have large flower heads with stiff, straw-like, radiating bracts of white, yellow, pink and brown, while others have several small flower heads clustered into a larger head.

RIGHT: Steedman's honey myrtle *(Melaleuca steedmanii)* is native to Western Australia. Growing to about 1.5 metres, it has papery, spongy bark.

RIGHT: The insect-catching sundew *(Drosera* sp.) has glands which exude a sticky substance, trapping insects which are then digested by the plant. The substance glistens in the sun like early morning dew. Growing in moist, acid and boggy areas, these plants are found throughout Australia.

OVERLEAF: State emblem of South Australia, the striking Sturt's desert pea *(Clianthus formosus)* brightens dry inland Australia after the rains in spring and summer.

ABOVE: A member of the mint family, snake bush *(Hemiandra pungens)* is a prostrate shrub native to Western Australia. The attractive bell-shaped lilac flowers appear in spring and summer.

BELOW LEFT: Poverty bush, or common emu bush *(Eremophila glabra)*, from Western Australia, grows to a height of 1.2 metres and has a distinctive downy, greyish white stem. Flowers, which attract honeyeaters, are borne in leaf axils throughout spring and summer.

BELOW RIGHT: Found in the drier parts of Western Australia, the native foxglove *(Pityrodia terminalis)* has soft, felt-like leaves and tubular flowers.

OPPOSITE: A profusion of creamy pink flowers adorns the common fringe myrtle *(Calytrix tetragona)* during spring. Belonging to the eucalypt family, this group of shrubs is found throughout the country, with the majority growing in Western Australia.

OPPOSITE: Gold dust wattle *(Acacia acinacea)* has masses of golden flowers in spring and summer. Growing to a height of 2 metres, it is found mainly in southern and south-eastern Australia. There are over 600 species of wattle distributed throughout the country, with shapes varying from low, spreading shrubs to upright trees.

ABOVE: Golden wattle *(Acacia pycnantha)* is found in New South Wales, Victoria and South Australia. Wattles are found in every part of the country from the well-watered tropics to the arid centre and cold mountain regions. They are pioneer plants, often the first to appear in bush fire-ravaged landscapes.

CENTRE RIGHT: Closely related to the kangaroo paws, sheath conostylis *(Conostylis vaginata)* is found in the Albany and Esperance areas of Western Australia. These plants are spring flowering and resemble the Japanese iris in their growth habit.

BOTTOM RIGHT: Native to Victoria, rough mint bush *(Prostanthera denticulata)* has aromatic foliage and purple tubular, lobed flowers.

ABOVE: The candle-like flowers of chenille honey myrtle *(Melaleuca huegelii)* appear in summer. Native to Western Australia, this bushy plant grows to about 2 metres. Melaleucas are commonly known as paperbarks in tree form and honey myrtles in the smaller forms.

LEFT: The robin redbreast bush *(Melaleuca lateritia)* is another Western Australian native, growing to about 2.5 metres. The botanical name for this genus means black and white, thought to refer to the blackened lower bark and white upper bark of some species resulting from fire.

LEFT: Graceful honey myrtle *(Melaleuca radula)* grows to about 2.5 metres and is also native to Western Australia. Melaleucas are often found along watercourses or swamp edges and in open forest, woodland and shrubland.

OPPOSITE: Probably the best-known and widely cultivated shrubs, callistemons are generally found in open forest and woodland in relatively high rainfall areas. The yellow-flowering *Callistemon pallidus* grows to about 4 metres and is native to Victoria and Tasmania.

LEFT: Sandheath bottlebrush *(Beaufortia squarrosa)* is spring flowering with attractive bottle-brush type flowers produced at the ends of the branches. Beaufortias are found only in Western Australia. There are 16 species, all of which are shrubs with fine, small, stiff foliage and flowers varying in colour from mauve, through brilliant reds and oranges to deep maroon.

BELOW: A summer-flowering variety, heath bottlebrush *(Beaufortia orbifolia)* grows to about 2 metres. Beaufortias are closely related to melaleucas and grow in sandy and gravelly soils in low rainfall areas. The genus was named for Mary Somerset, first Duchess of Beaufort (1630–1714), an early and enthusiastic patron of botany.